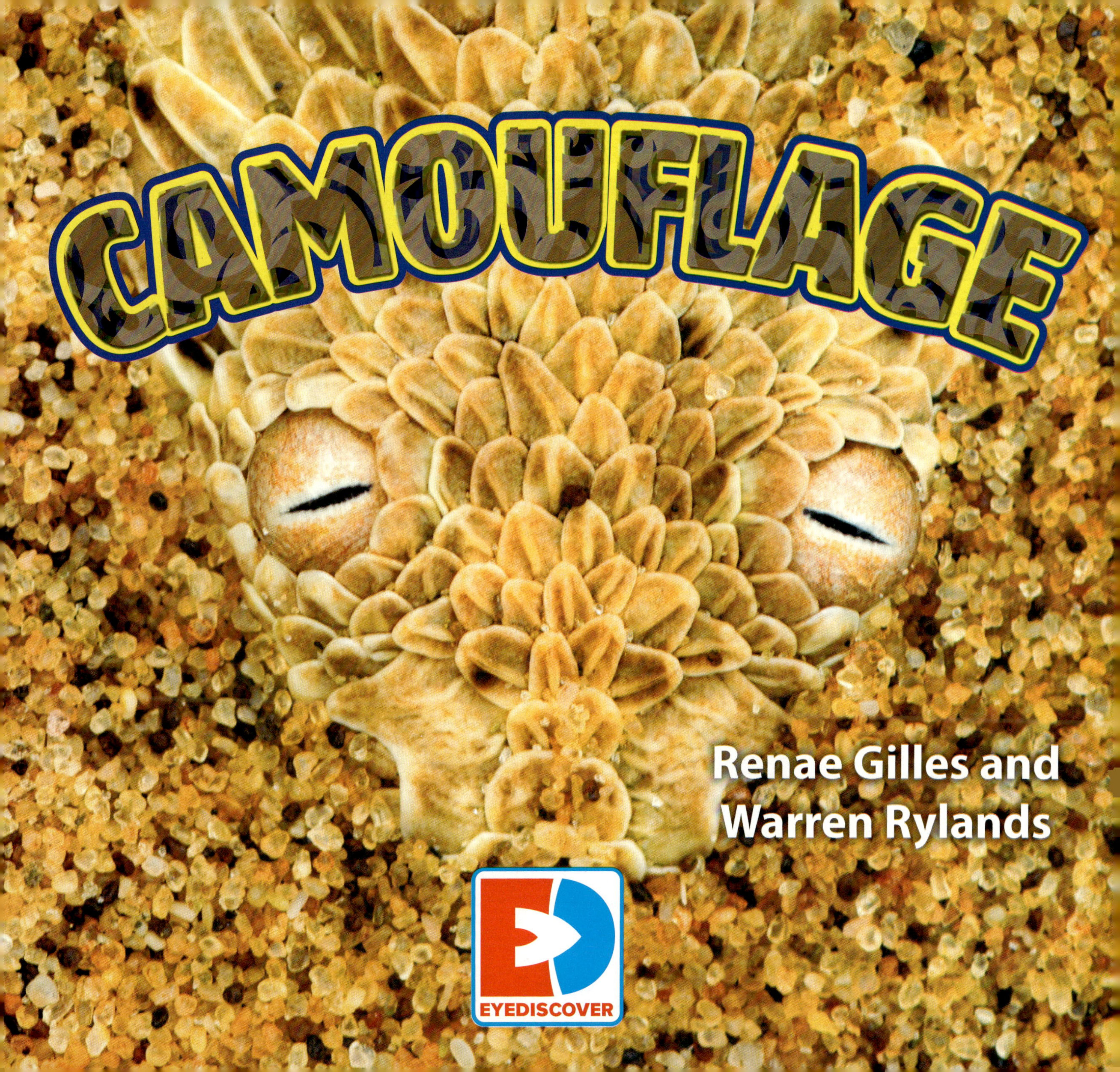
CAMOUFLAGE
Renae Gilles and
Warren Rylands
EYEDISCOVER

Go to www.eyediscover.com and enter this book's unique code.

BOOK CODE

AVM47456

EYEDISCOVER brings you optic readalongs that support active learning.

Published by AV² by Weigl
350 5th Avenue, 59th Floor New York, NY 10118
Website: www.eyediscover.com

Library of Congress Control Number: 2018951107

ISBN 978-1-4896-8017-4 (hardcover)

Printed in the United States of America
in Brainerd, Minnesota
1 2 3 4 5 6 7 8 9 0 22 21 20 19 18

082018
120917

Project Coordinator: John Willis
Designer: Mandy Christiansen

Weigl acknowledges Alamy, Getty Images, and iStock as the primary image suppliers for this title.

EYEDISCOVER provides enriched content, optimized for tablet use, that supplements and complements this book. EYEDISCOVER books strive to create inspired learning and engage young minds in a total learning experience.

Watch
Video content brings each page to life.

Browse
Thumbnails make navigation simple.

Read
Follow along with text on the screen.

Listen
Hear each page read aloud.

Your EYEDISCOVER Optic Readalongs come alive with...

Audio
Listen to the entire book read aloud.

Video
High resolution videos turn each spread into an optic readalong.

OPTIMIZED FOR
- ✔ TABLETS
- ✔ WHITEBOARDS
- ✔ COMPUTERS
- ✔ AND MUCH MORE!

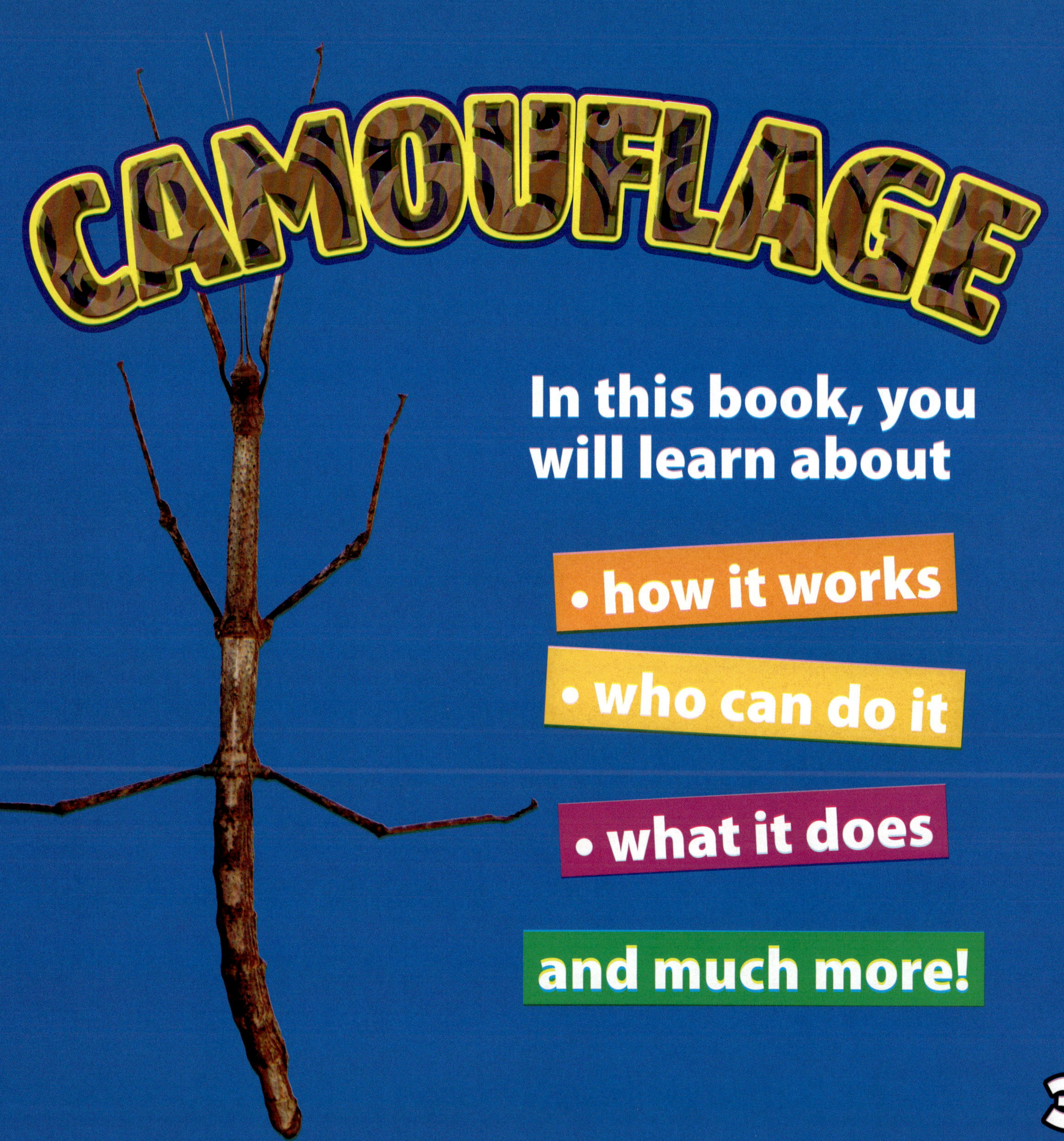
CAMOUFLAGE
In this book, you will learn about
• how it works
• who can do it
• what it does
and much more!

Camouflage is when an animal's colors help it hide.

6

The animal's color and shape may match where it lives.

Color patterns can make it hard to pick out one animal in a group.

10

Camouflaged animals can hide from other animals that want to eat them.

Camouflage can also let animals sneak up on what they want to eat.

Some animals are able to change their colors.

Many animals have fur that changes color through the seasons.

Other animals can change color in seconds.

Millions of animals use camouflage. It is important to help protect them all.

CAMOUFLAGE BY THE NUMBERS

The **arctic fox** is the only dog that **changes colors**.

A **cuttlefish** can change into **14** different **color patterns.**

An **octopus** can change colors in less than **one second.**

A **zebra's stripes** stand out to people, but not to lions. Lions are **color blind**.

There are **50** kinds of **insects** that look like **leaves**.

A **cheetah** has **3,000** spots that help it hide.

KEY WORDS

Research has shown that as much as 65 percent of all written material published in English is made up of 300 words. These 300 words cannot be taught using pictures or learned by sounding them out. They must be recognized by sight. This book contains 42 common sight words to help young readers improve their reading fluency and comprehension. This book also teaches young readers several important content words, such as proper nouns. These words are paired with pictures to aid in learning and improve understanding.

Page	Sight Words First Appearance
4	an, help, is, it, when
7	and, may, the, where
8	a, can, group, hard, in, make, one, out, to
11	animals, eat, from, other, that, them, want
12	also, let, on, they, up, what
15	are, change, some, their
16	have, many, through
20	all, important, of, use

Page	Content Words First Appearance
4	camouflage, colors, hide
7	match, shape
8	patterns
12	sneak
16	fur, seasons
19	seconds
20	millions, protect

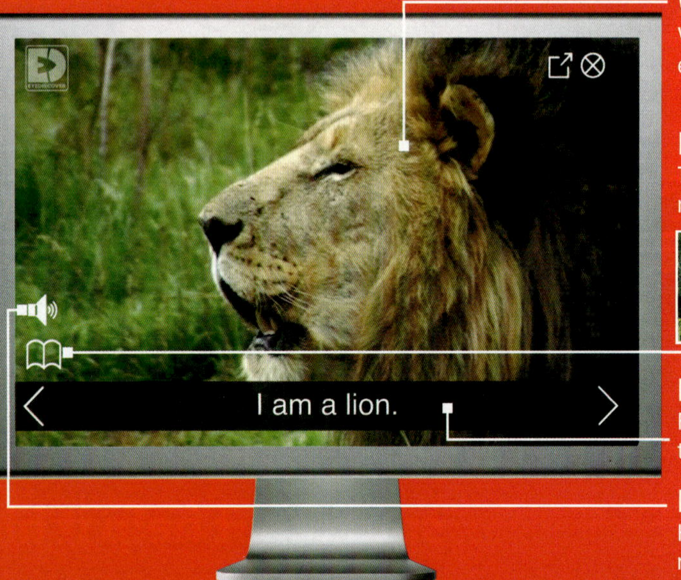

Watch
Video content brings each page to life.

Browse
Thumbnails make navigation simple.

Read
Follow along with text on the screen.

Listen
Hear each page read aloud.

Go to www.eyediscover.com and enter this book's unique code.

BOOK CODE

AVM47456